Andre Curse

A storybook about recursion

by Omi M. Inouye

Dedicated to Audrey Vaughan

who made a book for my sister where the pages were made of cloth and there were pockets filled with things to snap to the pages.

You could tie a shoe, button a button, and count the spots on a ladybug.

I learned that books could be more than words on a page.

...and that my oldest sister got all the cool presents.

ISBN-13: 978-0-9878239-0-8

How to finish making this book:

If this is a brand new book, it is not quite done yet!
You will need to cut out these 13 coloured tabs -->
(or visit www.omionline.ca for printable tabs and tips on preventing rips).
The number in the white portion of the tab is the number of the page that the tab goes on. Line up the white part of the tab with the dashed box on the page and attach the tab with clear, easily adjustable tape. The right hand tabs can be attached as you read the book, however, the bottom tabs must be placed before you start the book.

How to read this book:

If you read this book in order from the first page to the last page, it won't make a lot of sense. Instead, you must follow the pointer arrows. Every right hand page has a box in the lower right corner. Follow the pointer arrow coming out of that box. If the arrow points to a tab, flip that tab fully (if the tab started on the left side, it should be on the right side after the flip, or if it started on the right side, it should be on the left side after the flip), and start reading again on the left most page.

When Andre learns something new, move the tab on that page such that the writing on the tab is sticking off the page. Do not flip that tab. Always follow the arrow coming out of the lower right hand box.

If you find it difficult or annoying to move the tabs, attach the tab to the dotted box on the right hand side of the page and fold the tab in so that it is not sticking out. When Andre learns something new, unfold the tab.

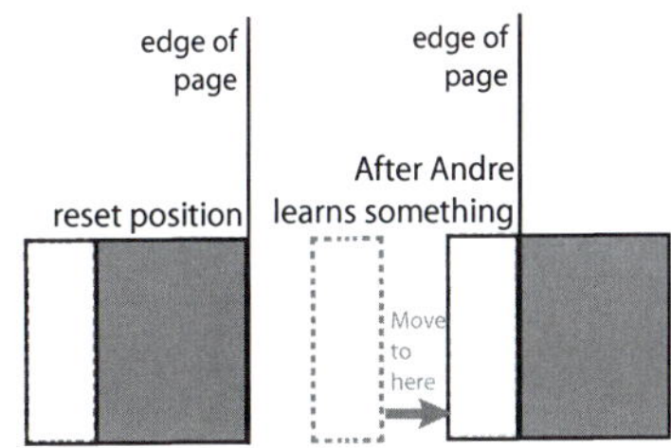

Visit www.omionline.ca for replacement tabs.

page 27	page 12	page 16	page 17	page 11
How to spell my name	Andre Curse	Home	Yes	No

page 31	English
page 35	Literature
page 41	Math
page 45	Physics
page 49	Chemistry
page 55	Music
page 65	History
page 67	Everything!

This arrow means turn the page.

This is Andre Curse.

Sometimes he felt like he was cursed with boredom.

It seemed like he just sat around all day with nothing to do.

But then early one morning, his mother called him...

“Andre Curse!”

"It's time to go to school," Andre's mom said.
"Mom, do I HAVE to go to school?" Andre asked.

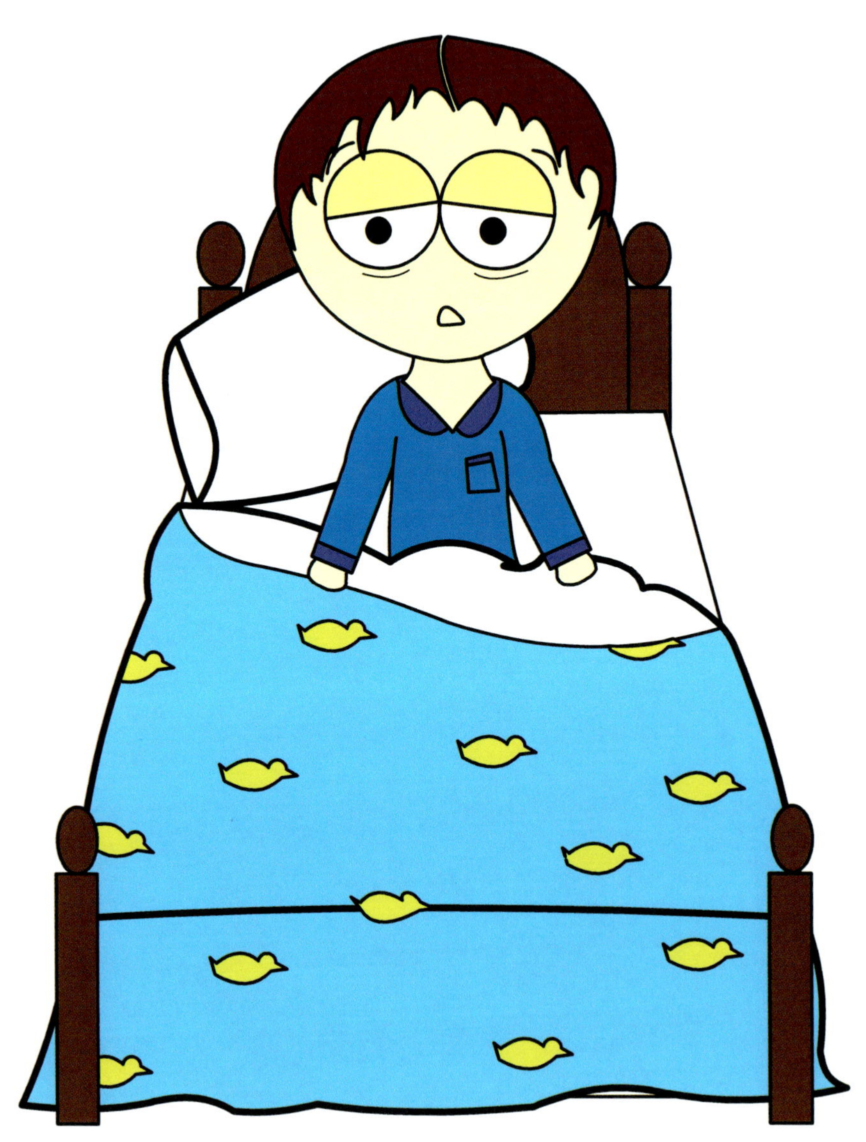

"I already know..."

"So do you know everything yet?"

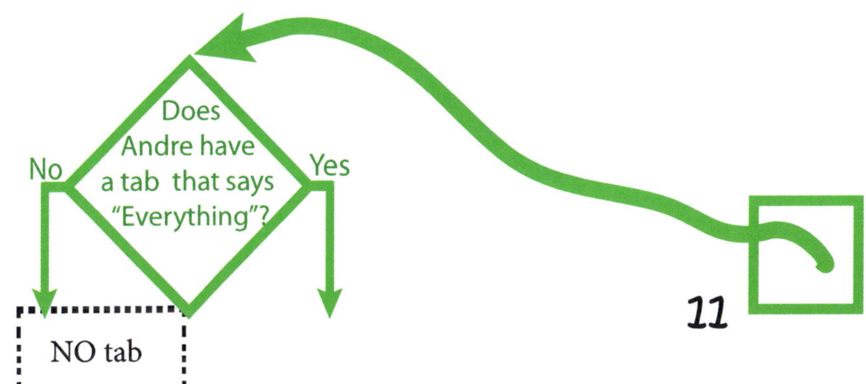

"Andre, there's so much more to know."

So Andre went to school.

(Flip the lowest tab)

It had been a very long day so Andre went straight home to bed.

He slept all night.

But then early the next morning...

"Andre Curse!"

HOME tab

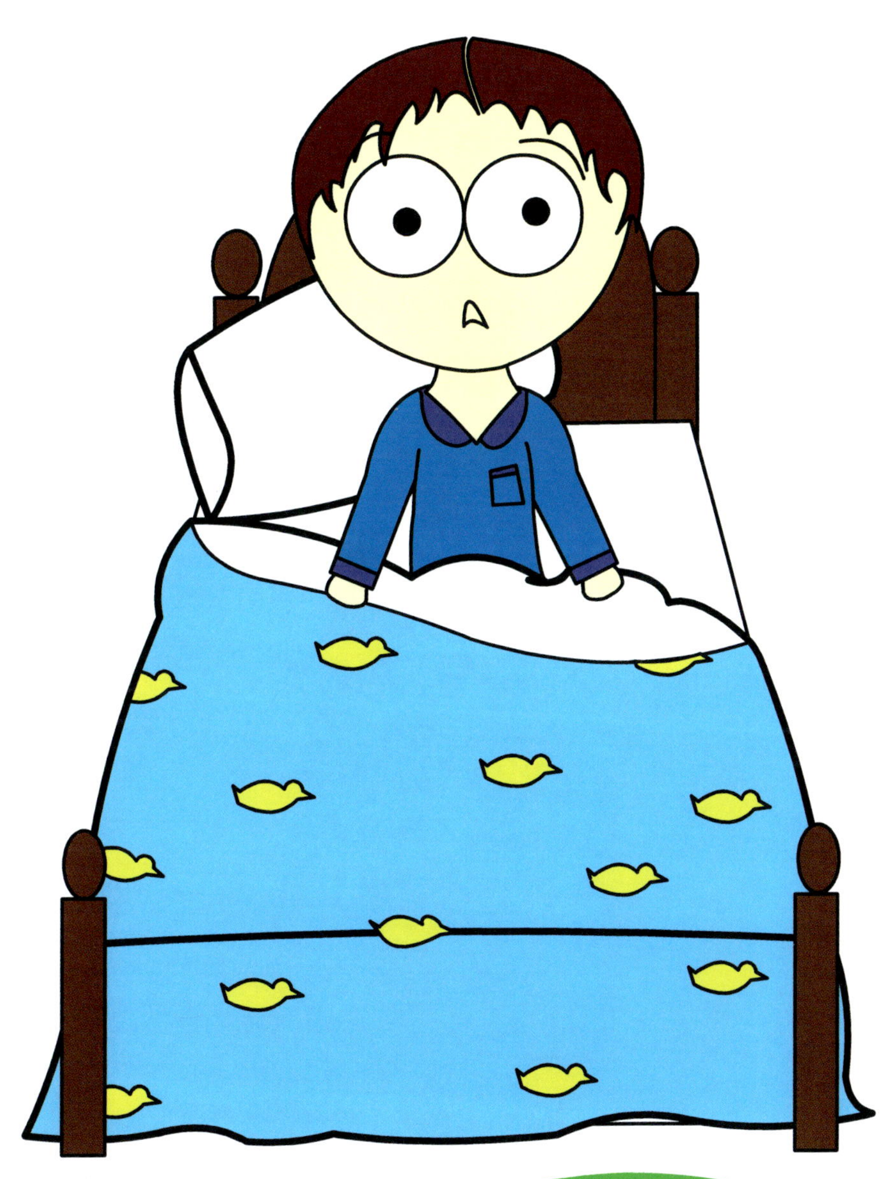

YES tab

"Andre! You know everything! I'm so proud of you!"
His mother gave him a big hug.
"I guess you don't have to go to school today!"

So Andre went outside and played baseball.

He wondered how far the ball would go if he hit it from the moon.

So he got some paper and a pencil and worked it out.

The End

```
import java.util.LinkedList;

public class AndreCurse {
	public static LinkedList<String> curriculum = new LinkedList<String>();

	public static void main(String[] args) {
		String [] subjects = {"English", "Literature", "Math", "Physics", "Chemistry", "Music", "History"};
		LinkedList<String> andreKnows = new LinkedList<String>();
		for (String c : subjects){
			curriculum.add(c);
		}
		AndreCurse(andreKnows);
	}

	public static void AndreCurse(LinkedList <String> andreKnows){
		if(andreKnows.contains("Everything")){
			System.out.println("Andre knows everything!");
			playBall();
		}
		else{
			String subject = curriculum.getFirst();
			goLearn(subject, andreKnows);
			AndreCurse(andreKnows);
		}
	}

	public static void goLearn(String subject, LinkedList<String> andreKnows){
		andreKnows.add(subject);
		System.out.println("Andre learned " + subject + "!");
		curriculum.remove(subject);
		if (curriculum.isEmpty()){
			andreKnows.add("Everything");
		}
	}

	public static void playBall(){
		System.out.println("Andre is playing Baseball!");
	}
}
```

Don’t forget to reset the book by moving the English, Literature, Math, Physics, Chemistry, Music, History, and Everything tabs back in. The other tabs stay where they are.

Special Thanks to:

Sarah Inouye, a Chemist
Tristan Inouye, a Farmer
Daniel MT Wood, a Mii Artist
David Schmidt, an Aerospace Engineer
and
Jonathan Schmidt, a Computer Engineer

oMii by Daniel MT Wood

Omi is a doodler, a ranter, and occasionally a computer scientist. When asked why she chose computer science, she normally answers, "Because recursion makes me laugh."

Omi is a self-referential acronym for Omi M. Inouye.

Omi is also the author of *Introductory Calculus for Infants* and *A Girl's Guide to Dating a Geek*.
For incoherent rants (not meant for children) or to contact Omi, please visit her website: www.omionline.ca

STOP NOW
(Or risk getting stuck in a loop)

He learned all the letters in the alphabet.

And he learned lots of words and how to spell them all correctly.

He learned about prepositions.

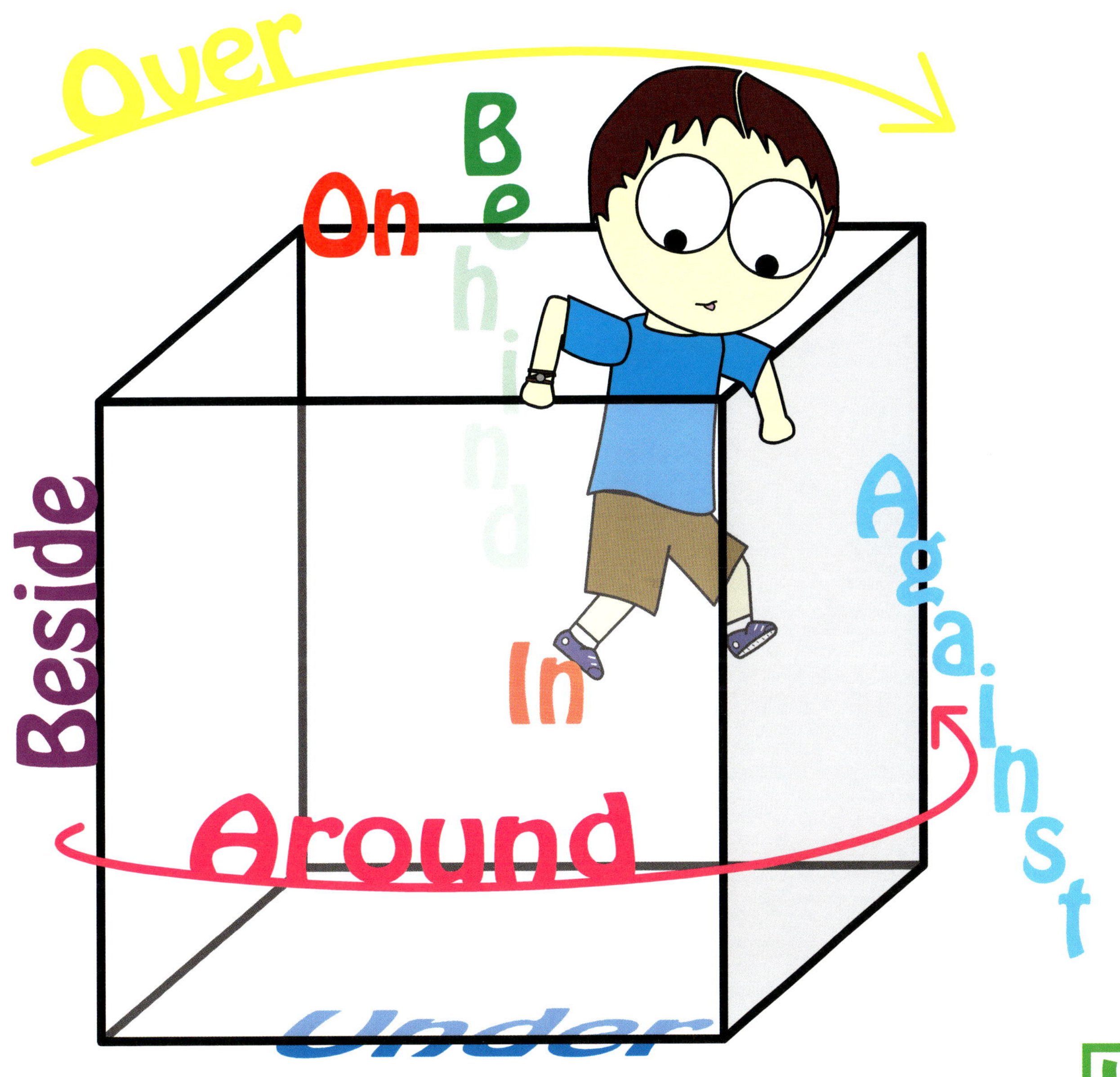

He learned about verbs and nouns.

NOUNS
-people, places, things

VERBS
-actions

Then he learned that a noun was a noun but a verb was not really a verb.

At the end of the day Andre's teacher said, "Congratulations Andre! You get an A+ in English!"

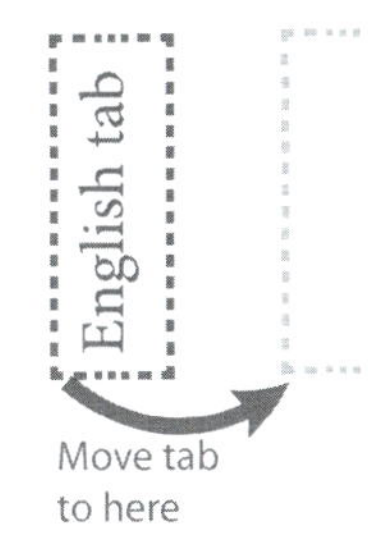

And she sent Andre home.

He read epic tales and short haikus.

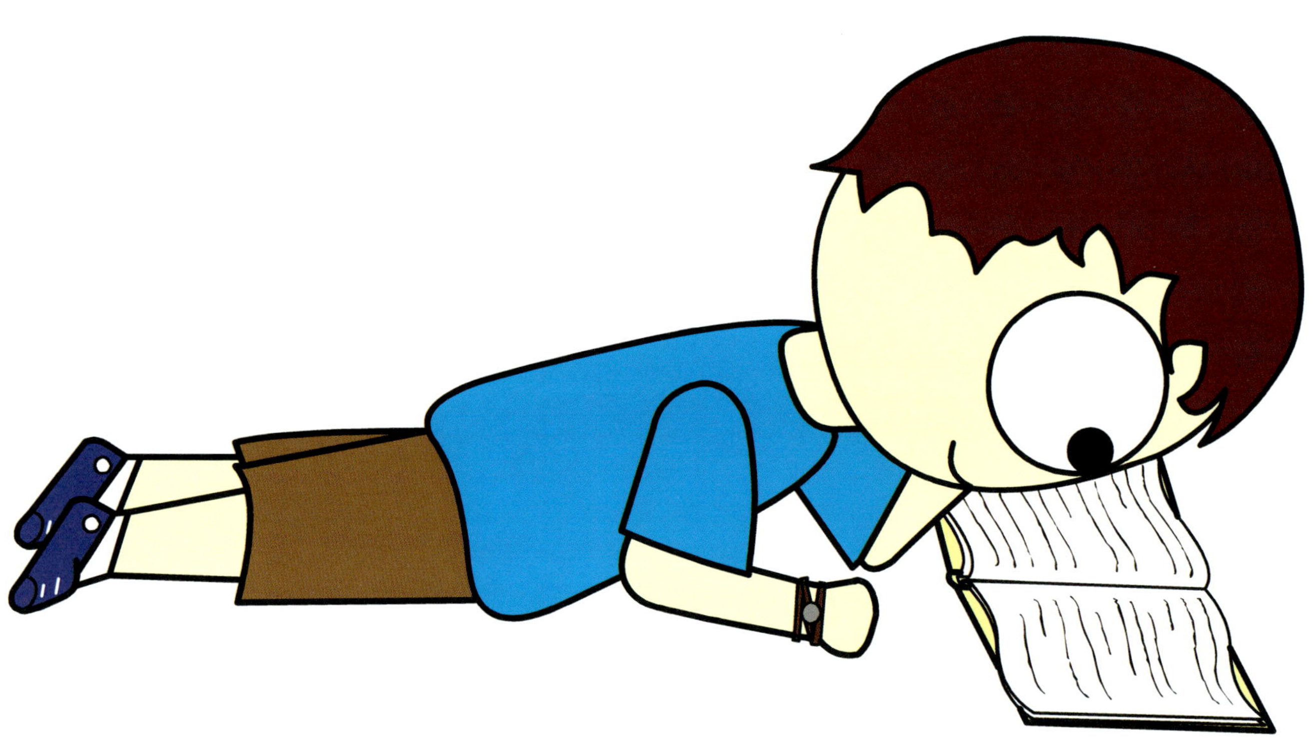

He learned about ballads and sonnets,
and he wrote some rhyming couplets.

He learned about introductions and conclusions and all the bits in between.

When he finished learning all these things, his teacher was very proud.
'Andre, you are completely literate in Literature now!"

And he sent Andre home.

He found out that he couldn't learn ALL the numbers but he still learned a lot of them.

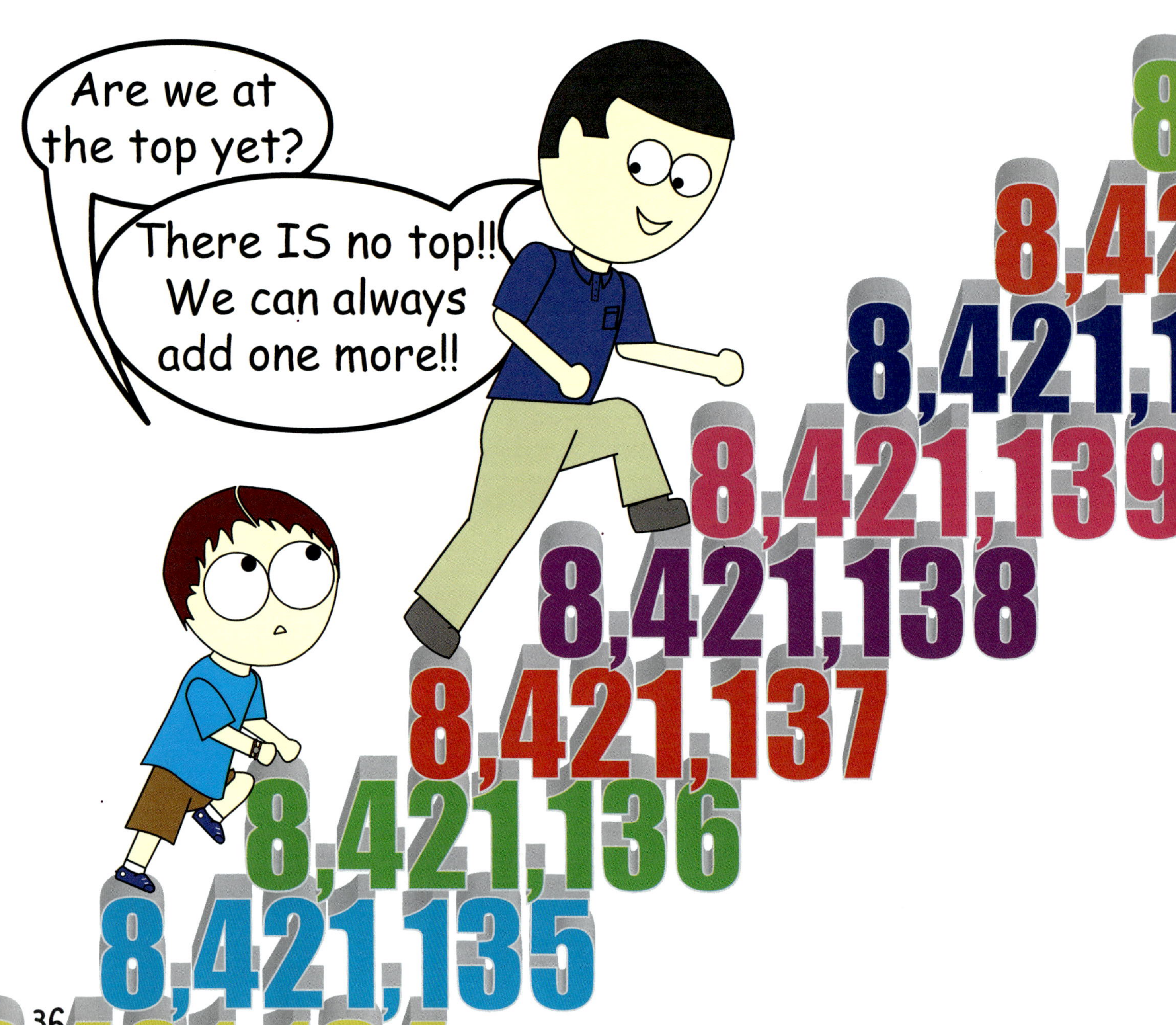

He learned about number lines and he learned how to add and subtract.

Then he learned about fractions and decimals.

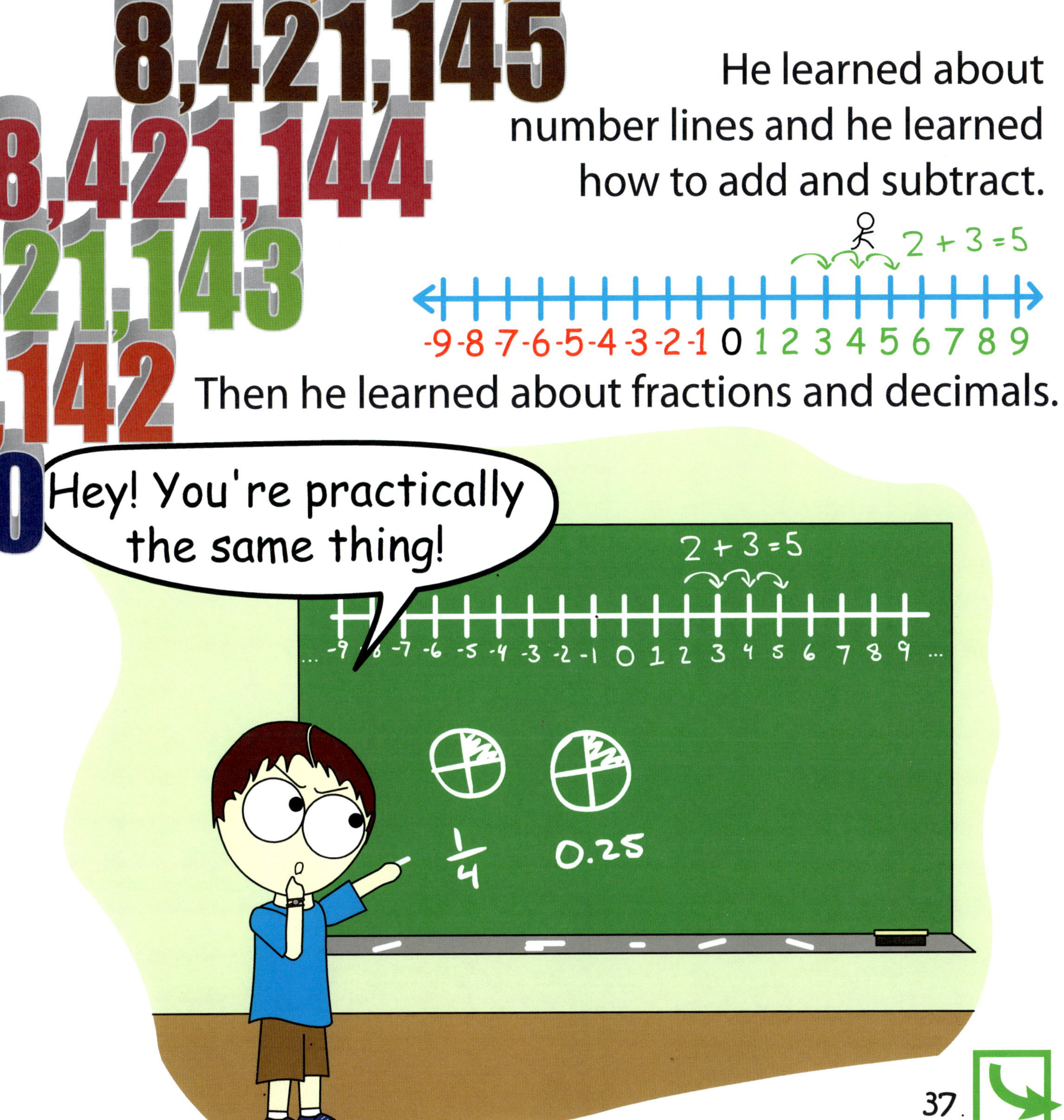

He learned how to multiply, divide,
and take powers.
And then he learned the correct order to do
them all in.

He learned that you can't square root a negative number...

...and then shortly later he learned that you actually could if you had some help from imaginary friends.

He learned Geometry, Calculus, and Algebra until his teacher said, “Andre! You get 100% in Math!”

And he sent Andre home.

He learned about motion and friction
and he learned about gravity and weight.

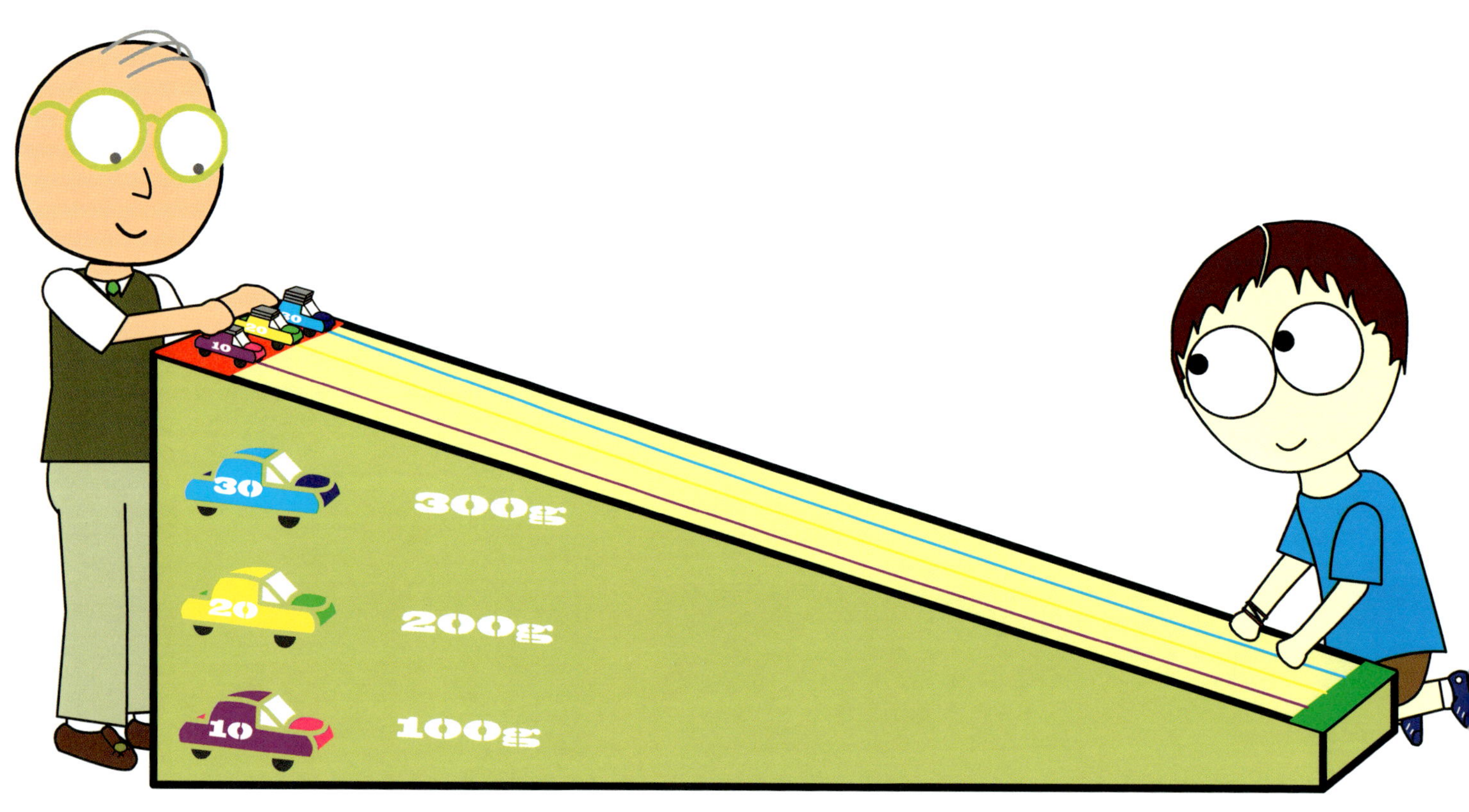

He learned about charge and energy.

He learned great words like oscillation, equilibrium, and pendulum.

"Andre, you show great potential in Physics!"
His teacher said.

And he sent Andre home.

He learned all the names of all the known elements.

He learned about bonds and got to make some cool models.

He learned about acids and bases.
And he performed an excellent titration.

Then, after he submitted his lab report, his teacher gave him a gold star in Chemistry.

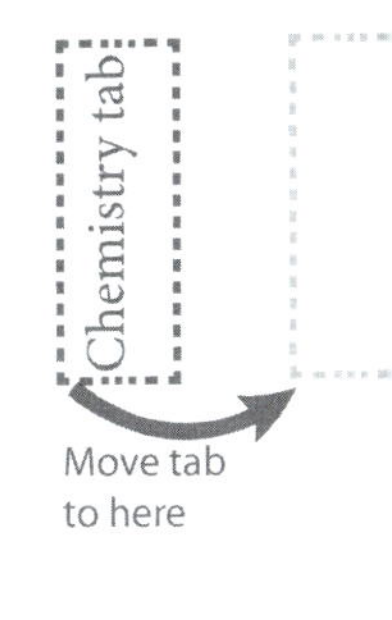

And she sent Andre home.

He learned about half notes and treble clefs.

He learned that letters could be sounds.

He learned that a symphony of a hundred people could lull a child to sleep...

...or that a single musician could fill a dance hall.

Then he learned how to play the drums because he learned that it was fun to be loud.

"Andre! That's enough!" His teacher shouted.

You are a maestro of music
and I think you should
go home. NOW!

Music tab

Move tab
to here

So Andre went home.

He learned about knights and peasants.

And he learned about exploration.

Andre learned that sometimes bad people tried to do bad things and that sometimes other people had to step up and say that wasn't ok.

His teacher said everyone should know their country's history.
So Andre learned a lot about beavers.

He learned that by using Math and Chemistry and Physics, people could go to the moon.

Or send a probe filled with pictures and music deep into outer space.

He wondered if there were aliens out there somewhere...

...and he wondered if they were
learning about
symphonies too.

Andre realized he had also learned about imagination, which wasn't on the curriculum but was still a pretty good thing to know.

Andre's teacher was very impressed.
"You've passed the past with flying colours!"

Move tab
to here

Then all his teachers came over and shook his hand.
"You know everything we have to teach you!"

Then they sent Andre home with a diploma and a cool-looking hat.